MW00617158

UNCOVERED

True stories of sex, God, and grace

Compiled by Julia Ann Pearson

PUBLISHED BY CAMERON PRESS
PALM BEACH GARDENS, FL

© 2011, Julia Ann Pearson
Published by Cameron Press
Palm Beach Gardens, Florida

All rights reserved. No part of this book may be reproduced in any form without written permission from the publisher. Exceptions are brief quotations embodied in articles or reviews.

Pearson, Julia Ann

ISBN 978-0-615-47561-5

Cover design: Dave Mozdzanowski
Interior design and typeset: Katherine Lloyd, The DESK

www.TheBookUncovered.com

Printed in the United States of America

Dedication

This book is dedicated to all of my friends who so
courageously *uncovered* their stories from such an intimate place.
Your willingness is beautiful, and I know that God will honor it
in lives that you won't even know that you have touched.
Thank you for giving of yourselves.

Acknowledgments

To my Heavenly Father—for this crazy plan you had for this book that I didn't even know about! You are so good and so big, and I love that!

To my parents, Marty and Laurie Berglund—who invested and loved in order for me to know Jesus, which changes everything.

To my husband Jeff Pearson—who waited so patiently for me in purity, and whose purity I still cherish to this day, and who is my most precious gift.

To my friends—who were so willing to step out and share their truth in Christ.

To my babies—who I pray one day can lay all the details of their lives, including purity, down at the feet of Jesus.

To Lynn Guise and Cameron Press—for seeing and feeling the importance of this book.

Contents

Preface

We live in a world of contrasts. While there is no dispute that our children and teens are bombarded constantly with sexual messages, most of them are hearing nothing about it from the adults who care about them.

As a Young Life leader, I have learned that the parents who have really discussed sex with their children are in the minority. Sure, there was the impersonal, distant "talk" that was dreaded by both parent and child. Certainly there were those who handed out condoms or birth control pills. Others gave their children purity rings and some religious instruction. Beyond that, I have heard of very few candid and open discussions.

Before I had children, it mystified me why parents didn't just talk to their children about a topic that was everywhere around them. Now that my husband and I have two children of our own, I have to admit that I break into a cold sweat at the mere thought of being honest, real, and transparent with them about sex, let alone discussing my own experience with the subject. Even considering this type of conversation is painful in and of itself. Just the fact alone that my beautiful little Ruby Rivers may one day not only need to hear about this topic, but possibly be interested in it—someone please slam me over the head with a meat mallet because, frankly, that would be a lot less agonizing!

Yes, I am starting to see why even the best parents, youth leaders, teachers, counselors, pastors, and other caring adults are so reluctant to be honest with the young people in their lives. Giving a raw account of their own past sex lives and what they have learned from both their good decisions and their mistakes is too hard. It's too real. It's too deep.

I have also come to see that one of the biggest questions that caring adults ask themselves is, "What if sharing my experience gives the young person I love a license to make the same regrettable mistakes I did?"

It is a terrifying thought.

On the other hand, I feel sad when I think about what my friends and I might have learned if someone had dared to be candid and vulnerable and humble about the choices they made and the results of those choices. That is why when it came time to talk about sex to our Young Life teens, I felt so passionately about talking frankly to them. I made the decision that I would lay it all out there, sharing the mistakes as well as the smart decisions and good choices. I wanted to help them steer clear of the pitfalls, and I also wanted to point them towards a good path. By telling my story, I knew that they would be able to see the consequences of my good and bad choices.

So, I told my story. My husband Jeff told his story. Our "kids" reacted positively, and I decided that the risk had been worth it. As time went on, I became concerned that we only had those two stories! Certainly there had to be many in the group who already could not relate to our stories.

And then, one night, God gave me a bigger idea!

I don't know if you have ever experienced an idea that felt as if God had smacked it into your heart, but that was what it felt like to me. I became completely and utterly engrossed in following what He had told me to do.

I began to ask adults who I knew truly cared about young people to share their sincere, real stories of how God's plan for sex has played out in their lives—good, bad, ugly, and beautiful.

As I look back, I can see that I was operating in something I call "turbo God idea mode." I could not be bothered to stop and think about all of the wounds and scars and embarrassment that I was asking my friends to share.

Despite my brashness, my friends responded in excitement and passion. They became as eager and intent as I was to tell the truth in order to share what they had learned. For many, it became a hopeful thought that God would make something beautiful out of their failings.

So, my friends and I all went there together, and uncovered it all, and that's what this book is—a big pile of uncovered journeys. Each one is diversely intricate, yet all end in the exact same way—GRACE. More than anything, I hope that you see that the reason so many different journeys could lead to the same end is because my friends and I all have the same Father in God, who gives each of us His GRACE.

My prayer is that as you read these stories, you will respect each of my friends for being willing to give the gift of vulnerability to you. I pray that you will learn something new and original from every single story, something that will give you a better understanding of yourself or of those around you. I pray, too, that there is at least one story in this book that will touch your heart in a deep, consequential way that will transform the way you see yourself, your choices, and your loving Father.

This book is offered to you by many with love.

Julia Ann Pearson

one

JULIA PEARSON'S STORY: I GAVE AWAY PIECES OF ME

From an early age, I learned from my home and my church that sex was something sacred and reserved for marriage. When I turned 14, my parents took me out to a fancy restaurant and gave me a purity ring. They talked to me about saving myself for my future husband and how this was part of God's perfect plan for sex in our lives.

As I got older, I remained true to this promise to God, myself, and my parents. It was hard at times because I felt like the pressure was huge in the world around me, but I felt confident in the young woman God had made me to be and the kind of man I knew He was saving for me. I was proud and excited about my commitment and my future.

I do however feel that I made some pretty stupid mistakes in some pretty silly relationships in high school. I had been boy crazy since the second grade, and, of course, that carried through into high school. I didn't have a ton of boyfriends or a million random hook-ups, but I did fool around in some ways I wish that I hadn't. It was never out of a feeling like I needed to please anyone or keep anyone around, but more out of my own curiosity and sense of adventure. Deep in my heart, I knew I was pushing some boundaries, but I rationalized it by comparing myself to all of my friends who were doing so much worse. I would always reassure myself that at least I was not having sex. Looking back now, I really wish that someone had talked to me honestly about how remaining pure meant setting up a lot more boundaries than just not having sex.

As I moved from high school to college, I really took a hard look at myself and my personal boundaries. I started to think a lot more about the kind of man that I wanted to have as a husband and the kind of relationships I wanted to have in the future and what they would look like sexually. I started to think more about purity and how much I desired full purity for myself and for my future husband. I prayed and reflected and decided that I needed forgiveness and new resolve for my future relationships.

God is so good. He gave me grace and strength in my relationships in college. I only had a few boyfriends in my college years, but those relationships ended with a very different feeling than I had in the past. I was proud of the purity kept in those relationships.

For Jeff and me, our story of purity is pure and simple. Jeff knew from a young age that he wanted to remain pure until marriage. His decision was not made because of his parents or his church, although those were factors, but rather because of his personal relationship with God and his strong convictions. In his relationships with girls in high school and college, Jeff never did more than kiss. He always treated girls he dated with the utmost respect.

When Jeff and I finally got together, we established very strong boundaries from the very beginning of our relationship. We had been close friends before we started dating, and we knew that we both had saved ourselves for marriage. That was really important to us, and now that we were dating, we had to figure out how remaining committed to purity was going to play out in our relationship. We both knew that this meant much more than just not having sex. We made a commitment not to do anything beyond kissing, and even in kissing, we would be careful because we didn't want to let lust into our relationship.

Of course, this was hard. To be honest with you, though, when you are in a good relationship with another Believer who is truly committed to purity, a relationship that is based on your relationships with Jesus, a relationship where both of you are thinking "this is the kind of person I want to marry," it really isn't as hard because you are focusing on God and on how sweet the end reward will be.

Jeff knew that I had a few things in my past that I wasn't proud of, and I knew the time would come when I would have to really hash it all out in honesty. I will never forget the night when we were dating when I told him about every guy that I had given a little piece of myself that I wouldn't be able to give Jeff for the first time. I cried, and Jeff cried, and then I cried harder. I remember the hurt I felt knowing that I had been so selfish. In all my "fun and adventure," I had only been thinking about myself. I was not thinking of Jeff. I was not thinking that one day I would find a man that I loved with all my heart and wanted to give all of myself, and I wouldn't have all of it to give. All of it was important. All of it was priceless, and now I saw the hurt that I had caused the one man that mattered.

It was hard for him, but Jeff gave me grace, and I had to remind myself that God forgave me a long time ago when I had asked for His forgiveness. Now I needed to forgive myself, and we both needed to move on from there.

Jeff and I got married more than six years ago. During our wedding that my dad performed, I gave my purity ring to Jeff. It was a really beautiful moment for Jeff and me and my parents. That day, of course, was the best of our lives, and that night was sacred and beautiful and fun! Jeff and I felt so blessed to be able to give each other that huge gift of our virginity, and neither of us can imagine what it would have been like without that precious gift. Getting to know someone sexually that you love so intensely is so amazing and a never-ending adventure. It is so intimate and holy, and I cannot imagine cheapening it in a relationship that is not forever.

That is my story. I am giving you this very personal look at my life because I want you to choose God's best for you. I have asked other Believers to share their stories. All of us pray that God would give you strength in your journey to follow Him with your heart, soul, and body.

two

I HAD NO SELF-ESTEEM

I was sitting in Art History class. It was my sophomore year. Gary came in and sat next to me. In the small Christian college I was attending, everyone knew Gary. He was in the "cool" group—athletic and very good looking. Since I was not in the "cool" group, Gary had no idea who I was, but he started talking to me. I knew that Gary had a girlfriend, but I was spellbound from the first sentence.

As the weeks went by and I saw Gary in class three times a week, we talked a lot more. After class one morning, he asked me if I wanted to get coffee. I loved hearing about his life, what he liked, what he didn't like. He liked looking at my homework and talking about himself. I see that now, but I didn't see that then. I just saw his appearance and couldn't believe he would pay any attention to me.

I was (and am) a Christian. I had gone to a Christian high school, and now I was in a Christian college. Of course, I had heard from my family, my school, and my church that sex was for marriage only. That was God's plan. I had every intention of following all of God's plans for my life so I didn't give it much thought at all. I had dated in high school, mostly going to youth group events, but a kiss here and there was about it. Again, I didn't think much about it. I had not considered any boundaries or alarm bells.

After the first coffee "date," we started hanging out with each other after class at least once a week. I never knew when it would be so I always kept my schedule open. Of course, I should say that I saw these as "dates," but I'm sure he never did. As I said, he was in a very serious, long-term relationship. Like many girls, I thought I could change that, and I could be the one. I lived to be with Gary.

Eventually, our coffee dates turned into trips to his off-campus apartment that he shared with three roommates. There was always at least one of the guys there, and we would all talk and laugh, and I felt important to be with them. They knew that I was helping Gary with his homework.

As much as Gary became my whole life, I knew that I couldn't talk about it. I would see him everywhere with his girlfriend, and he would barely acknowledge me. I didn't care. I thought that would change.

After a few months, we were given the class assignment to go to a museum. Gary casually asked me if I wanted to go to the museum with him and do the assignment together. I said yes. After we went to the museum, Gary stopped at a parkway rest stop, and he kissed me there.

Soon we were going to private places a lot, and the kissing progressed to much more. At this point, he never took me to his apartment. We never had coffee on campus anymore. Except when we were in class together, Gary barely acknowledged me. When he wanted to "take a drive," I had to walk to an off-campus spot where he would pick me up.

It was very easy for Gary to talk me into having sex with him, and we began a relationship that was only sexual for him, but it meant everything to me.

The semester was over, but we were still seeing each other on our "drives." The day came when I told Gary I was pregnant. He told me that he wanted me to get an abortion. He took me there, paid for it, took me back to school, and never called me again.

6

It's hard for me to write this story, but I know that there are many girls like me out there. I gave up the close relationship I had with Jesus (temporarily) for a false relationship with Gary. I would have done anything for him, and I did. I am writing to ask you not to find your self-esteem in a guy who doesn't care about you—except maybe for your homework and easy sex with no commitment. You're better than that. There is a guy who will love you for life, and he deserves all of you. Stay close to Jesus.

God has been good to me. I have a Christian husband and three children, but I have regrets that I thought so little of myself. I am a daughter of the Living God. I didn't live like it.

three

I MADE A BIG MISTAKE

I have had boyfriends since I was in middle school. At first, my boyfriends were the ones you sat next to in the lunch room and held hands with in the hall while everyone giggled as you passed. I was raised in a Christian home, and when I got to high school, my parents gave me a promise ring that I was to give to my husband on our wedding night. I made a vow to keep myself "pure" for my husband.

In high school, I only had two boyfriends. With one boyfriend, we never kissed or were alone together. We followed God's way, and to this day, we are still friends. At the time, however, I often thought our behavior was stupid and restrictive because everyone else was "having fun." Now looking back, I can see the wisdom in our behavior. I had no idea the effect that my emotions could have over my physical body. The second boyfriend was about four years older than I was, and he pushed me to go further. At first, I was able to say no, but the more I cared for him, the more I wanted to please him. Thankfully, I made it out of that relationship with only going as far as heavy kissing, but I was convicted that was wrong.

College was a new experience for me. There were freedoms that I never knew existed! Boys and girls could be in the same room, go on trips, and spend the night at the same houses off campus. At first, these new freedoms did not affect me. I didn't have a boyfriend and so it did not matter. Halfway through my freshman year, I started dating a senior named Roy. He was very popular and charismatic and wrote me letters every day. Every time we had a date, he would send me a card through campus mail filled with the kind of sweet things that make girls sigh in sappy love movies.

By my sophomore year, I was completely in love with this man! We had even talked about marriage. At this point, Roy had graduated and was living in a house off campus. We spent a lot of time there together. We watched movies and played video games with his roommates. On Halloween night, we were watching a movie alone in his room. One thing led to another and thanks to my naive view that I wasn't going to let it go that far, I failed, and we ended up having sex. I was mortified and told him we couldn't date anymore. I couldn't believe that even with a Christian background, a promise ring, supportive parents, and all of that, I did the very thing I promised I would never do.

Roy and I grew apart fast after that, and a few months later, we broke up for good: so much for marriage, so much for my own strength, so much for my promises. I should have been giving my love to God first, and I should have given my whole body to His keeping. He doesn't ever let anyone down.

Girls, don't underestimate your emotions when it comes to a man! When you love someone, you think you will be with them forever and you want to hold onto them by giving yourself to them. That's a big mistake. Don't be confused: sex does not equal love, and love does not equal just sex.

God is good and forgiving, and I am married now to a wonderful man who saved himself for me. Telling him what happened between Roy and me was the hardest thing I have ever had to do. Imagine telling a man who loves you that you once gave another person a part of yourself that you will never get back and should have been for him.

Thankfully, Tom continued to love me the way that God calls a man to love a woman. He supported me even when I told him he deserved better. We have been married now for five years and have two beautiful children.

I hope that you can see from my story that if you have failed in your attempt to stay pure, don't feel hopeless! There is hope with God. Don't feel unlovable! God still loves you and is willing and able to turn all things to "good for those that love Him." 🖐

four

I MARRIED THE ONE WHO WAS HAND-PICKED FOR ME

I started loving Jesus at the young age of five. I also started loving boys fairly soon after that! I was very much your typical boy-crazy girl.

I vividly remember getting my heart broken for the first time at a summer camp at the young age of 11. I was crying in the bathroom when a pregnant mom walked in. She comforted me and shared with me that God had someone hand-picked just for me and he would be my soul mate. She encouraged me to start praying for him now, to pray for him to love Jesus and to save himself for me and me alone.

That's exactly what I did.

Enter the awkward teen years. I was still faithfully praying for my future husband. I prayed for growth in his spiritual walk and that he would stay pure sexually for me. As time went on, I also added in a few physical features of my own choosing: blond hair, blue eyes, athletic—a soccer player would be nice!

Of course, I was praying, too, for my own faithfulness to my future husband. This was not a problem whatsoever since there were zero prospects for a boyfriend—or at least any I wanted to be my boyfriend! I had high standards. I knew I wanted to marry a man who loved Jesus so why should I waste my time dating anyone who didn't? I never looked twice at a boy who was not a committed Believer.

When I was 16, two of my youth group girlfriends and I bought little silver purity rings. We made a promise to God and ourselves that we were going to stay pure sexually for our future husbands. I wore that ring faithfully on my left ring finger and was not embarrassed to tell people what it meant.

I decided to major in Athletic Training. Within the first week of school, I was assigned to work with the men's soccer team where I met my future husband: a soccer-playing, Jesus-loving, blond-haired, blued-eyed hottie! We started dating in October of our freshman year.

During the dating years, I learned that he was also a virgin (cha-ching!), but unlike my non-existent prior dating life, he was quite "the man" in high school. He had many girlfriends and opportunities for sex but was able to resist them all. I know without a shadow of a doubt that my faithful prayers for him from the early age of 11 kept him from giving himself away during the height of the sexual temptation teen years.

During our four and a half years of dating, we made a commitment together not to give up our virginity until marriage. It definitely wasn't easy, and I can recall many heartaches trying to keep that promise. But, God gave us the strength to have sexual boundaries that were not crossed. On the night before our wedding, wrapped up in a sterling silver box, was my promise ring that my soon-to-be husband would receive from me.

Now married ten years with two beautiful children, I can honestly say that our sex life is still strong and passionate. I believe God rewarded my celibacy and faithful prayers with a wonderful sex life and an unselfish lover. My advice to you would be to pray continually for your future mate! Pray for his/her love for Jesus and for his/her purity. And don't waste your time dating a non-believer or even a non-growing Christian. You might miss the prize God has hand-picked for you—someone who might just be praying for you. 🪔

five

I WAS A TYPICAL GUY

G rowing up as a typical teenage guy, sex was always on my mind. I began dating in the seventh grade and used these dating relationships purely as "hooking up" opportunities. The more I dated, the further I went sexually with my girlfriends.

Now, there was a difference between me and most of my guy friends. I was raised in a religious home, and a message of purity was instilled in me from my parents and youth leaders at church. Of course, in the heat of the moment, those messages were not as loudly heard!

Girlfriends would come and go, and hearts would be broken, but, of course, that was typical for the teenage years. I tried to push the boundaries as far as my girlfriends would let me. By the tenth grade, most of my guy friends had already had sex. None of them was in a serious or committed relationship.

I had pretty much done everything sexually by my sophomore year except I had not had actual sexual intercourse. That was the one thing I did not push for, and, remarkably enough, my girlfriends didn't either. It is interesting to note that especially in high school it was the girls who usually pushed for that—often as a way of legitimizing the relationship.

I vividly remember one particular night when I was at a friend's house with our girlfriends. We had all been drinking and having a good time. My girlfriend asked me if I had a condom. The pressure was on, and the excitement was building, but there was also a small voice in my head and heart asking me to really think about this:

Would I have any regrets about this decision later tonight?

What about the next day?

How about the next year?

What about if and when we broke up?

Then I began to think about my future wife, and I asked myself:

Would I want her to be doing these things with her boyfriend now?

All of those questions were swirling in my head as I heard my girlfriend say, "Don't worry about the condom. Let's just do it."

A guy's dream come true! Except for me, it was not. In some ways, it was my worse fear being realized. A real decision actually had to be made—in the heat of the moment!

I knew it was a decision that would stay with me for life and would change me forever. I can only attribute God and my parents for the decision I made, but to this day I am glad I made that decision. Nothing further happened that night or the next or the next.

Eventually we broke up and a rumor began circling about me that I didn't want to have sex. Friends speculated about the reasons. Was I gay? Did I have something physically wrong? Was I some sort of religious nut? None could understand or comprehend why a guy like me would not want to have sex.

I must be honest. Those months were difficult. However, eventually we all leave high school and all of the high-school drama behind us and move on.

My college years were amazing, and I grew in maturity and confidence, no longer caring about what others thought of me or trying to live up to certain cultural expectations.

I found the girl of my dreams and actually began a serious relationship. We were both committed to keeping our sexual purity until we found our spouses and got married.

Well, it just so happened that I married her, and I will never forget the amazing feeling and blessing knowing that we cared enough about each other to wait for sex until our wedding night. I can add that it was totally worth it!

I recently attended my 10-year high school reunion, and it brought back many memories. It is remarkable how many of my friends remember my stance and now reveal to me just how impressed they actually were but could not admit that at the time to me or others.

One friend told me, "Allen, I wish I had the courage you had back in high school. That would have saved me from so much pain, confusion, and consequences."

Personally, I have yet to meet someone, whether religious or not, to tell me, "I wish I had more sex with more people growing up."

Conversely, more and more adults confess to me that they wish they could have waited until they found the right person not only to share their bodies with, but also to share their hearts and lives as well. Unfortunately, it often takes experiencing negative consequences to understand how important the decisions we make in our early years actually are.

I am glad I did make that decision to remain sexually pure (as hard as it was) and am thankful that to this day I have no shame, guilt, or regrets. 🖐

SIX

MY PURITY WAS STOLEN FROM ME

I t was the night before I was to leave for my freshman year at college. My boyfriend of several months picked me up to swim and hang out at his parents' house before I left. We had fun together and then he was supposed to drive me 10 minutes back home—except that he pulled off into a deserted quarry and raped me.

Of course it was my fault, right?

I never bothered to have the conversation with him that I was a virgin and had no intentions of having sex with him. I knew that he had already had sex previously with at least one other girl at school. Couldn't I have screamed "no" louder? I didn't tell a soul and tried to bury the whole shameful, disgusting thing into the deepest part of my mind that I could. I felt like damaged goods. What "good" guy could ever want me now? How could God forgive me?

I spent my college years subconsciously believing that I had to "put out" if I were to have any hope of a relationship. I told myself that was what guys needed and then maybe there would be a chance that they could love me. I wanted to be normal and be married one day and have kids. Now how could that ever happen?

I settled for someone who was not good for me, but at least he wanted me. We spent about ten years together until he finally proposed.

There were a lot of great things about him, but there were also important things that were very wrong. The major one being that I did not have first place in his life (that spot was already taken by his mother). He belittled me, and we would argue about too many things.

Our relationship was not rooted in Christ. I didn't realize it at the time, but God was there all the while sending me so many signs that this was not His choice for me. I called off the wedding, knowing that making that decision could mean I would end up alone.

What a mess. If I had only talked to someone and to God, it would have saved me a lot of heartache and wasted years.

In His time, He has blessed me beyond belief. I have the most loving, understanding, forgiving God, and I am now married to a loving, understanding, and amazing husband. As I look back, it is so clear how God has used this ugly thing and turned it into something beautiful. I am so humbled and thankful to finally realize that all the time I shut Him out, made bad decisions, or tried to do it my way, He was still loving me and gently calling me to know Him more. Despite what happened to me and how I mishandled it, He loves me and desires to know me and forgives me and died for me. That is the only love I need.

seven

I AM WILLING TO WAIT

When I was first asked to write my story, I thought it really might not be best for me to be giving advice on a subject I've never experienced. The more I thought about it, though, I realized that's exactly the point. I've now gone through eighteen years of my life without even a kiss, a date, or a boyfriend. Of course, I'm not saying these are things you should necessarily avoid. Young love can be a great experience, I'm sure. However, God doesn't have those plans for me right now, and I'll just wait for my time to come.

I know it would have been easy for me to just find someone when I was feeling alone. I have several friends who were in similar situations and found solace in hooking up with guys that didn't really care about them just so they could have the feelings of someone wanting them. However, I never wanted a one-night stand or to be wanted for just an hour. Call me a hopeless romantic, but I desire the love that makes your heart soar and makes you feel alive.

Sometimes it's weird to be one of the only virgins in my group of friends. It feels like I'm missing out on something so important. I'm not going to lie. Sometimes being alone hurts a lot, and I question myself. You hear all about the guys, the experiences, and the satisfaction your friends have had. However, when it all comes down to it, sex remains a mystery in my mind. My friends who chose to have sex with just anyone are the ones left with emptiness and more loneliness than before. My friends who "saved" themselves for a boyfriend they "loved" ended up heartbroken as they were dumped two weeks later.

As for me, I'm completely content with my situation. Especially now at college, I know it'd be so easy just to find a guy that would be interested, but the problem is most just want one thing, which I'm not willing to give.

Although it's hard sometimes not to know the thrill of your first kiss or how perfect the world could feel with someone else's hand in yours, I'm willing to be patient. As for now, I refuse to give myself up for just some random guy at a party, for I know God has something amazing waiting for me. 🐚

I WAS DESPERATE TO KEEP HIM

Sex. This simple little word holds so much value. Its value is something I have not always treasured the way God intended for me.

I became a Christian in high school and, of course, started learning about the boundaries God set for us for sex. I read books, did Bible studies, and talked with my youth leaders about it. I felt like I had a pretty clear understanding of what Jesus wanted for me when it came to my body and giving it away to a man. Sex was—for so many reasons—a gift that I needed to cherish until my wedding night when I could give it away to the one He brought into my life.

And then I went to college. And then I met Ron.

Ron was charming. He was cute and funny and seemed to think that I was the greatest girl he'd ever met. Ron wrote me cards and letters, put CDs in my car of songs that reminded him of me, took me home to meet his family, and stayed up all night talking to me when he had class at 8:00 the next morning. I was Ron's princess—until another girl caught Ron's eye, and he went running to her. When Ron got tired of her, though, he always came back to me. This was a cycle that lasted all through college. Each time Ron came back to me, I think I was more and more desperate to keep him there, and I was willing to do whatever it took.

The day came when I gave my body to Ron. I cried and cried after

23

it was over. I couldn't believe I had just done what I had vowed to keep sacred until my wedding night. It didn't stop there, though. Ron and I slept together a few times after that, and each time left me feeling more and more empty.

Finally, I had to cut Ron out of my life because the damage he was doing to my heart was just too much. Not only did I feel like I was losing my Ron that day, but I was losing a part of myself as well. The most precious part of myself that I had to offer, I had given to him and now I was saying goodbye.

After Ron, I dated some other guys who I knew from the start were not who Jesus wanted for me. Most of them were not Christians, and, yes, most of them wanted sex to be a part of the relationship. At that point I thought, "Well, I've already ruined myself. What's the point in holding out now?"

I cannot even begin to express how wrong I was in my thinking and the heartache and pain that have followed my decisions. I have dealt with physical repercussions as well as emotional. I have felt the shame and emptiness of giving everything I have to give to a man and not having that cherished. The heartache is indescribable.

My point in telling you all of this, though, is not to just preach about saving yourself for marriage. The other side of my story is about healing. It took the greatest heartache of my life to bring my eyes back to Jesus. I have realized that it is only through His mercy and grace that I can be made whole again. For so long, I thought I was "damaged goods" and that no man of God could possibly want me after all I had done.

Jesus is teaching me, though, that this is simply not true. He is making me whole again, and along with the pain, there is so much joy and beauty that comes with the healing. I know that God will bring a man into my life who is going to love and cherish every part of me. That man will do everything he can to protect my purity—and on my wedding night, I will make love for the first time. 🐚

nine

I SHARE A GIFT WITH HIM AND NO OTHER

I can say from personal experience that it is worth the wait.

We did date for a long time—eight years! I knew early on that I wanted to save myself for my husband, and it was something I took seriously. At times, it was hard to wait, but from the start we drew definite boundary lines. It was important for us to make those boundaries outside of the moment. It helped us to get to know each other and not get distracted by the physical stuff. I think that was the biggest benefit.

We went to college together, and, at some point, we began to push our lines a little. We began to realize that our physical relationship was taking priority over the rest of our relationship. We decided to step back and not even kiss for a few months so that we could get back to learning to love each other in other ways. Our friends thought we were strange, but it was a great time for us.

I would also tell you that when you are dating, sex seems like such a huge deal, and it is everywhere and always in your face. In reality, it is only a small part of life—a great part of life if it is handled well but still a small part.

I have known people in relationships that revolve around the physical aspects, and they aren't healthy and often don't last. If a relationship is built on love for each other and love for God, then it has a good chance of success. When we were dating, we used to say often that it was our love for God that brought us to love each other. I think that is really important.

After eight years, that day arrived where we came before God and committed to love and cherish each other for the rest of our lives. Then we were able to give each other an amazing gift that we share with none other. It was totally worth it. In marriage, we have been able to learn about sex with each other and from each other.

ten

I AM VALUED BY GOD

I f you had asked me four years ago, I would have definitely said that I was a valuable person and that I deserved good things, but the way I lived my life communicated a much different picture. I am the girl who has had more experiences with guys than I care to admit.

Sadly enough, the first time I ever had sex was at the young age of 15. I gave away the most precious gift of my virginity to a guy who couldn't possibly have understood the value of the gift I gave him. At the time, my idea of love had been shaped by the deception of fairytale romances in books and on television. I didn't have a clue as to what love was. The only thing sex did for me was bond my heart to an immature guy who didn't stay in my life very long.

At age 19 in college, I started dating Jake. Being so close to Jake left me particularly vulnerable to a long period of mental abuse from a guy who was controlling and jealous. I didn't want to break up with Jake, though, because I wasn't sure if I could do better, and I thought we were in love. Eventually I ended the relationship. As my junior year progressed, I began to live a little more recklessly. My friends and I headed to the bar often, and when we went out, guys were on our radar.

When I look back at college, I realize I wasted so much of my time chasing after guys. While I was quickly spinning out of control and giving pieces of myself away, I unfortunately didn't realize that there was a thin line between lust and love so I confused the concepts quite easily. Plus, the idea that a solid friendship without sex between a guy and girl could actually be an amazing foundation for a good relationship was an unknown concept for me and my friends.

In 2006, I went through a very difficult breakup with a guy who I had been in a serious relationship with for more than two years. He was someone I had grown close to beyond a superficial level, and he was the first person I ever realistically considered marrying. But unexpectedly, he dumped me for another girl, and the breakup was more difficult than any trial I had faced. I couldn't eat or sleep. It was hard to get out of bed in the morning. It was the beginning of some deep reflections in my life, and it was one of the first times I had ever really reached out beyond my friends and family and called upon the name of someone whom I had never asked for help from before. I called out to God.

I couldn't help feeling like I needed God in that difficult time. I also wanted an answer as to why God would allow something so painful to happen. Nothing made sense, but at the same time my heart kept telling me God was somehow involved in this whole situation. I just wasn't sure how.

A good friend invited me to the beach for a week, and I went. Going on the trip was great because it refocused my attention, but it also allowed me to meet Chris. Chris, like me, had just come out of a relationship and a difficult breakup so we immediately connected and were inseparable most of the trip.

After returning from the beach, we started dating. Chris was amazing, and as I got to know him, I realized he was a hundred times better for me than any guy I had ever met. After a year and a half of dating, I was almost sure Chris had gotten an engagement ring, and I was ecstatic. However, something inside of me felt off, and I had no idea what it was. In quiet moments, I searched out what I was feeling until I realized God was tugging on my heart. It was the strangest feeling because it was almost as if God was chasing me, and no matter where I went or what I did, His presence was there. The last time I had even really acknowledged God's presence was almost two years earlier after my breakup. Once that hurt and pain passed, I seemed to forget God was even there. Regardless, I made a decision to go back to church, but this time I would try to find a church that read from the Bible.

Sunday rolled around, and as I sat in the pew of the small church I passed every day on my way to work, I listened to the message and was reminded of the things I had learned as a child. God was the creator of the heavens and earth and all people. God was a loving God, but because of a sinful nature we are born with, we are eternally separated from God. However, God had made a way to remedy the broken relationship by sending his Son Jesus to die on a cross in order to pay the penalty of our sins.

Although I had heard the truth in the past, there was something much different about this time. I felt I really wanted to know more about Jesus and have an actual relationship with Him. During the worship part of the service that morning, I gave my heart to Christ and began my relationship with Him.

My life started to change drastically in so many ways. I was learning so much about an amazing God who loved me. One of the more important changes in my life was how God changed the way I viewed myself and how I viewed relationships with guys. It took a long time to connect the pieces, but God in His gentle way began to show me so many things about who I was and where I had been. Not only did God help me to understand that He didn't judge my ugly past, but He also helped me see that my past didn't have to dictate who I was.

I felt like I had been freed from a ton of guilt.

After becoming a Christian, my relationship with Chris became very difficult. I loved Chris and I wanted him to know Jesus the way I had come to know Him, but Chris wasn't interested. As far as he could tell, I had lost my mind. I thought for sure he was going to break up with me the day I told him that I wanted to stop having sex. He didn't understand why, and trying to tell him that sex was something that was sacred and only meant for marriage was a hard thing to explain. Chris loved me so selflessly that he agreed to wait. Chris even made an attempt to come to church with me although it was far out of his comfort zone. Our relationship continued on for another few months, but it was rocky at best. I had come to learn that God meant for a man and woman to enter marriage only when they were on the same page mentally and spiritually. Chris and I were not on the same page spiritually. It strained our relationship so much that I finally decided, after much crying and heartache, to break up with Chris.

The hardest decision I have ever made in my life up until right now was breaking up with Chris. I gave up what I conceived to be everything I wanted here on earth for a promise of everything I could ever want and more in heaven.

I will never forget the day I sat in my bedroom with a heavy heart, crying out to God to give me strength to carry on in the midst of all my hurt and pain. I sat reading my Bible, hoping to find something that would comfort me, and God blessed me with a verse: "I will betroth you to me forever; I will betroth you in righteousness and justice, in love and compassion. I will betroth you in faithfulness and you will acknowledge the Lord." (Hosea 3:19-20)

God showed me through that verse that although I was no longer engaged to Chris, I was now betrothed to Christ, my first real "one and only." God whispered words of love wrapped in a promise of faithfulness that would never end.

I am still single and still struggle at times to accept that reality, but the momentary bouts of loneliness fade in comparison to the joy I receive from God every day as He teaches me about the never ending love and compassion He has for me. I forget about my own human desires when I read God's Word, and He reveals to me that He is intimately involved in my life and cares about who I am. God has an amazing plan for me, and I love learning about it one day at a time. 🎧

eleven

I TOLD MYSELF THAT EVERYONE WAS HAVING SEX

I grew up being told, "No sex before marriage." I followed that rule pretty closely up until my freshman year in college. I was dating a girl who was a senior in high school, and we messed around here and there. I told myself, "Well, it could be worse. We could be having sex, but we're not so this is okay." It's funny how that works, though. You say, "A little bit here and a little bit there," and the next thing you know, you've consumed the whole thing.

The dumbest part was that I used the excuse, "Well, everyone's doing it." I know now that wasn't the truth. So eventually, my girlfriend and I had sex a few times, and it wasn't anything like you see in Hollywood movies! It was actually quite disappointing. But the reason why I think it was so disappointing was because it wasn't something that was blessed by God. In other words, the sexual encounters God blesses are ones that are within a marriage covenant.

The other side of it is the whole emotional aspect of sex that people often miss. That's a huge part of sex—hence the term, "making love." It sounds lame, but it's the truth. I wasn't "making love" to my girlfriend. It was just fulfilling immature, lustful desires. Sex the way God designed it is so much more than just the act of sex. It's about souls connecting through the amazing gift that God gave us to enjoy.

After a lot of disappointment and heartache, the relationship ended. I am now married to the most amazing woman of my life. I am now experiencing the kind of sex that God intended. It's amazing! And I'm not talking about the way it feels physically. I mean, don't get me wrong, it's awesome, but I'm talking about connecting to another person in a way that's just beyond description. I wouldn't have been able to experience this kind of connection, enjoyment, and fulfillment with any of the girls I dated because it would've been outside of God's boundaries. Now I am truly "making love."

Do I have any regrets for my past decisions? I do! I gave away a part of myself to someone else who shouldn't have had it. It's like taking a beautiful gift, say like a brand new car, and beating it up. It's no longer shiny, and it's the farthest thing from perfect. Now imagine, taking that beat-up car and giving it to the most precious someone in your life.

That's how I felt going into my marriage. I felt like I damaged the gift of sex that God gave me. I couldn't fully enjoy the gift with my wife because I was trying to treat a rusty old car like it was a brand new Ferrari. It just doesn't work that way.

I am thankful that God enjoys taking things that Satan intended for evil and turning them around for good. That's what God has done for my marriage. Through great lengths of talking, praying, and forgiving, my wife and I are now able to fully enjoy the gift of sex that God has given us. 🕊

twelve

I WAITED FOR SEVEN YEARS

I t wasn't easy waiting for seven years to have sex with someone I loved, but looking back now, we would never change that decision.

Of course, we weren't able to put off having sex through our own strength. I'm pretty sure that's impossible for a seven-year period of time! It was only through Jesus and His gracious ways that we were able to stay strong. So my first advice would be to realize your weakness and then realize God's strength. He'll give it to you if you want it.

I remember one time one of my friends came to me asking for help because she and her boyfriend were getting more physical than they wanted to, but they didn't know how to stop. She said they kept trying to set up boundaries, but the boundaries never worked. The only thing I knew to tell her at that point was that the closer she was to God, the more she would want to please God.

Of course, there are other good things to practice, such as not putting yourselves in tempting situations. I do think, though, that it's about us and God. The question is, "Do I want to please my boyfriend or God?" Perhaps an even more important question is, "Do we both want to please ourselves or God?" If you truly want to marry a Godly man or woman, ask that question. Your boyfriend's (or girlfriend's) response will tell you so much about his (or her) priorities.

So after just a year and a half of marriage, I can say that we've gained an intimacy that I could have never imagined, and I can say that it's an intimacy that I've had with only one man. What movies and high school friends usually don't tell you about sex is that it's the most vulnerable thing you will ever do in your life. I always believed that God created sex to be shared between two people in a committed relationship, but now that I've actually had the experience, I understand on a different level why it is not meant to be spread around. Having sex outside of the safety, love, and blessing of marriage is in all likelihood only going to cause harm.

I can promise you this: You'll never regret waiting, but you'll probably regret not waiting. 🖐

thirteen

MY PARENTS' MARRIAGE MADE ME INSECURE

Joe and I waited to have sex until we were married. That is one of the most important decisions we will ever make. I truly believe God has blessed both of us because of it.

I was always so restless in relationships in the past. A big part of that was due to my parents' marriage not working. I just thought that I would never find the right person, and that was a very scary feeling to me. So when Joe and I dated for a year and a half the first time, I always had anxiety about whether or not he was the one for me—even though he was a great Christian guy. My restlessness led to our breaking up and spending a year and a half apart. In that time, I dated other people and, of course, the temptation to have sex was always there, but I knew that I had made that commitment to God and was determined to keep it. I knew that someday, even if it wasn't Joe, the right person would come along.

A year and a half later, Joe and I got back together. In the time we had spent apart, he had also dated other people. At first, I wondered if he had been able to keep the commitment to save himself. When we eventually talked about the time we had spent apart, he told me that he, too, had resisted the temptations around him and had kept his commitment to save himself for marriage.

We have a lot of friends who have had sex before marriage. The difference is huge. In fact, many of them have insecurities that I no longer have. I believe God is in control of our relationship, and He will continue to bless us. 🖐

fourteen

I LISTENED TO BAD ADVICE

Today's society glorifies sex without boundaries. The truth is that God created us with a purpose and a design. God created sex to be good, but at the same time, we often overlook that part of God's design is for sex to remain in marriage.

It is up to us to follow God's way or to suffer the consequences.

In 1 Corinthian 6:18, the Bible says, "Flee from sexual immorality." In 1 Corinthians 6: 20, it continues with, "Therefore honor God with your bodies."

A youth leader recently told me that sex is like a fire. It is nice and good in the fireplace, but outside of a fireplace it can be fun at first. However, it takes a quick turn to being dangerous and burning the entire forest down. As silly as that analogy may seem, it is completely true.

When I met Craig, I had recently begun my walk with Christ. I hadn't learned much about sexual purity, and I still had insecurities about myself. Craig helped me a lot and always complimented me even when I felt at my lowest. He never pressured me into doing anything I didn't want to do, and he respected my wishes about not having sex— even though at that point he had no plan to wait until marriage. We were on different levels so our relationship was often shaky and weak.

Craig and I were becoming more serious. Although he would never pressure me, I could feel pressure from others. People would tell me that I would lose him if I didn't have sex with him. They told me that sex is truly what makes a strong relationship. I was naive and fell into the temptation of believing that sex was necessary to keep a relationship alive in today's society.

However, I was very wrong. I had sex one time with Craig. Since then, I have been reading my Bible more. I know that I cannot reverse the past, and I understand how much damage I've done to my intimacy with God and others. I know what I have done is very wrong and is a sin. That is why I have asked for forgiveness and have been very open with Craig about how I wish to wait to have sex until I am married to the one I love.

I now plan on remaining sexually pure until marriage. In John 8:11, Jesus told a woman caught in a sexual sin to "go and sin no more."

Sex before marriage is wrong, and I advise anyone to please not make the same mistake I did. Do not be influenced by the "advice" of others. Sex doesn't strengthen a relationship. It was designed by God to be enjoyed only in marriage. Even if you feel like you are truly in love with a person and feel like you will marry each other, you should wait until marriage to have sex.

God loves us, wants the best for us, and that is His plan.

fifteen

I WAITED; HE DIDN'T

I f someone had told me ten years ago when I was seventeen that I would struggle through what should be a celebratory sexual relationship with my husband, I would have felt so cheated. Actually, I guess I am still working through those feelings. Bob and I come from two very opposite ends of the sexual spectrum. I grew up in a family that went to church, prayed a lot, did family things together (and actually liked it), and sought God for our lives. Each of us had our weaknesses, but we had genuine hearts to follow God. That was one reason why I accepted Christ when I was eight years old.

When I was twelve, I attended a youth conference and made another commitment to God but in a more specific way than I had done four years before. At that point in life, I had already been to a birthday party where I was pressured to drink and was already very aware that the temptations of the world would hit me full throttle in the upcoming years. I knew those temptations would stretch beyond just the pressure to drink beer: maybe cheating, maybe lying, maybe being fake—one person inside my home, another outside of it. For certain, there would be pressure to have a boyfriend and do, you know, "boyfriend and girlfriend" things. So, at twelve, I made a decision to make wise choices in the area of purity.

Of course I wasn't flawless in those areas as I grew up, but God definitely protected me. He allowed me to choose the narrow path, and at many times, it definitely felt very narrow and without much company. It was really hard for me not to date just anyone so as a result, I dated very little. I ended up feeling insecure. In addition to my own insecurities, the evil one told me so many lies: "You're just not beautiful." "Are you even attracted to the opposite sex?" "By the time you have a serious relationship, you'll have no experience, and it will fail." "No one finds you worthy of pursuit."

Those were tough battles of the heart to fight.

As I entered my later college years, I met those lies head-on. I became more aware of how God sees me and more confident that I needed only His admiration for true fulfillment. I reached a point in my heart where I said something like this to God:

"Lord, I don't know why You'd have me feel so different from many girls my own age. Since You haven't brought anyone into my life, I know my desire to have a boyfriend is really an empty desire. I've bought into the lie that if I had a boyfriend, I'd feel fulfilled. I know You're the only One who can truly fulfill me. Allow my heart to want only You. You've brought me to this point in life for a reason, and You know I long with all my heart to love someone and to be loved. I'll wait for Your best, choosing not to compromise and not to believe lies."

Around that same time, I remember talking with two friends who, like me, were committed to waiting until marriage to have sex. We were discussing what we thought it would be like to marry someone who had already had sex. We talked for a long time, and we each had different thoughts on what it would be like. One friend said she could not do it; she thought it would be just too difficult. The other girl thought it wouldn't be such a struggle because God provides grace, and we all make mistakes along the course of life. I remember throwing out some vague opinion because I'd never really thought about it. Plus, I'd never have to answer that question "for real." I just assumed that God would provide me with a husband who had longed for me and was so committed to Him that he would wait for me. I remember thinking, "No, no way. That couldn't be what God would want for my life. I've made a big sacrifice for whoever this man is. I've spent my whole life avoiding the mess that sex outside of marriage causes. I know You would not have kept me from that world only to bring me into it through someone else's past."

And then I met Bob.

During our engagement, it was difficult to think that I had waited my entire life to share physical intimacy with only this man, and now it would be different because he hadn't made the same choices. These issues took on a new dimension after we got married. As we got to know each other more as husband, wife, and sexual partners, the issues became bigger than several nights of "talking it out" could handle, bigger than time would heal, and bigger than any quick prayer in the morning would fix. We determined to be purposeful at seeking God to help us be honest and vulnerable with our sexual baggage.

After three years of marriage, I'm better understanding how in Christ Bob is free from his past. I need to allow him to have that freedom. Through all its challenges, God has been and will continue to make our intimacy beautiful.

I also understand more about my past. I understand that God requires holiness—defined as "being set apart"—for a purpose. I actually used to be embarrassed by my past because I felt like a little prude. I was really wrong. My decision to wait until marriage to have sex was not being a prude. God saved me from a life haunted by mistakes. I can't begin to describe how free it was to enter marriage as a pure partner, not having images in my mind to fight off from my past.

I look forward to sharing with my daughter that, yes, it's hard, but glorious freedom waits on the other side of refusing to compromise.

My husband's story is in the next chapter. 🕮

sixteen

SHE WAITED; I DIDN'T

Growing up, sex wasn't even on my radar at all until I was about a junior in high school. I started hanging out with a different crowd, and when I figured out what a sex life was all about, it was cool to think about the possibilities of having one. Having little direction from anyone older, I was left to learn from the people around me, and for them sex was like a trophy. I compare it to sports: you play to win; you date to have sex.

Sex for me at that time had nothing to do with affection or even showing you cared about the person. What was true about sex for me was so far from where God designs it to be. I guess the bottom line for me was that sex was for two things: the accomplishment and the feeling. Needless to say, I bought into the culture's lies. Everyone around me seemed to define sex this way so it was easier to buy into and live out.

I became sexually active later in high school with a girl I dated. I did care about this girl and had a friendship with her, but love wasn't even an idea at that point. Although sex with her felt physically good, it was not emotionally fulfilling at all. I felt empty. The act was most important. The relationship was selfish. If I had actually given it a deep thought, that feeling would have so paled in comparison to future consequences.

Before I even knew Him, God used a humiliating experience in college to change part of my future. One night when I had been drinking with friends, we were hanging out, and a girl I had casually known was among the group of people there. Basically, we were attracted to each other, and we ended up having sex. Afterward I felt really dirty. Although I knew who this girl was, she wasn't even the kind of person I would have been drawn to under normal circumstances. As suddenly as the experience with her happened was how suddenly the feeling of complete shame took over. I felt like I had defiled my body. Having sex with this girl seemed so much more pathetic because we didn't even have a relationship. I think that's what it was that made me feel defiled. I wished it had never happened.

About nine months later, I found Christ.

Everything in my life changed dramatically. How I viewed sex was no exception. Although I often felt unsatisfied while sexually active and knew it was wrong, there seemed to be little reason to stop. When I accepted Christ, He became the reason to stop—not because it was a rule, but because my heart understood the destruction I had caused to myself and to others. Among other commitments I made was the choice to date like-minded girls. In talking with a friend who had also recently accepted Christ, we decided together that, yes, we had made mistakes, but we would make Godly choices from that point on to salvage whatever was left for our future marriages. Even though God provided me with the strength and courage to keep that commitment, my marriage has been affected in deep ways as a result of my earlier choices.

After I accepted Christ, I battled what my mental picture of sex should be like. I had difficulty coming to terms with the idea that sex inside of marriage was meant to be beautiful. All I could associate sex with was the feeling of shame and defilement. I wanted to be so far away from how I previously viewed sex that I took a huge leap to the other end of the spectrum, which was just as inaccurate. Sadly, I never bothered to pursue God's intention for sex so I built up sheepishness toward the idea of sex. That sheepishness has tainted what God meant to be pure and completely untainted.

One struggle deals with understanding sex in emotional and spiritual terms. Before I was a Believer, my experiences with sex were non-emotional and non-connected. Inside of marriage, sex connects to *everything*. I understand that sex is good, and I love it but have really struggled to know how to connect my emotional, relational, spiritual, and romantic love for my wife with having sex. Since sex was only an act for me in the past, I have had difficulty understanding the magnitude of how our sexual relationship would impact all other areas of our marriage.

So many things are reminders of my past. I am frequently haunted by memories—what I did, how I manipulated girls, the selfishness that consumed me. It saddens me to think of the hurting people in the world who are suffering because of these same mistakes, and it's difficult to know that I've contributed to that pain. Although forgiven, I feel like I can't get truly away from my past.

Another consequence deals directly with my wife. Two truths I know: One, I am forgiven from my past totally and completely because of Christ. Two, I love my wife more than anything. What's even more difficult than any of my own baggage the past causes me is the pain I cause her. It breaks my heart to know that she is left to deal with the consequences of who I was before. I hate that she questions who she is as my sexual partner.

With God, there is hope, and He continues to strengthen our intimacy. But if I could do it over again, it would be so different. 🕯

seventeen

I JUST THOUGHT IT WAS WHAT PEOPLE DID

I became sexually active as a young teen and had basically no morals when it came to that part of my life. It was not that I walked away from what I knew was right. Rather, it was that I did not have any idea what was right because no one ever talked to me about anything like that.

Sex was all over the place so I just thought it was what people did. What I realized later in life was that I had absolutely no respect for myself and very little, if any, self-esteem. So to me, having sex made me worth something and helped me find self-worth for even just a short time.

It is really sad to think about it. I gave so much of myself away for nothing. Married now for almost six years, I think about how wonderful it would have been to say that my husband and I were each other's first.

We did wait until marriage for each other, which was nice, but there is so much baggage on my part that I wish would not be there. It does not go away very easily. There are memories and things to get over and get past.

Sex within marriage really is worth the wait. No one will ever regret waiting.

I will always wish I had waited. 🎸

eighteen

I MADE A FRESH START

My husband and I have very similar back-grounds in the area of sexual purity. We both came into the marriage having committed to secondary virginity. We each had been in unhealthy, long-term relationships and had made many mistakes—having sex being one of them. Both of us knew it was wrong. We felt horrible for having blown it in that way and repented and were so grateful for God's grace, for-giveness, mercy, and fresh starts.

Once we started dating each other, obviously the temptation was there; however, we were committed to waiting until our wedding night to share our bodies. Through God's strength and some awesome accountability partners, we did wait, and our wedding night was a beautiful celebration of how we knew God intended sex to be.

To any of you who have made mistakes or given yourselves to others in ways you regret, it is never too late for a fresh start and a new commitment. God is always ready and willing to pour out His cleansing forgiveness and mercy. Do not allow mistakes of the past to trap you in the present and take you down the wrong path for the future.

Remember that sex was God's idea. It was a good one. It is an amazing gift when enjoyed within marriage. That is how God intended it, despite what you hear and see all around you. It's okay to have questions. It's just not okay to get your answers from any source not in agreement with the Creator. 📖

I WANT TO TELL YOU ONE THING

I am 26 years old. My husband and I have been married three years. Both of us were virgins when we got married, and I cannot tell you what a huge blessing that has been in our lives and our marriage.

Sex is amazing and the most intimate thing you can do with someone. It is so great to be able to share that with just one person. I never have to worry that I'm not good enough for my husband or that he's thinking of someone else. I also know that I can trust him because he has demonstrated his faithfulness even before I knew him. This opens the door for healthy communication and marital intimacy instead of shutting it down.

There is so much that can complicate a marriage without bringing past sexual sin into it. The one thing that I want to tell you is that the less you do now, the more amazing it will be later.

I promise you that it's true. 🎧

twenty

I WAS SEXUALLY ABUSED

I'd have to say that I had a pretty skewed view of sex growing up. First, my parents didn't get along well, and they rarely, if ever, showed any affection. Second, and probably more important, I was sexually abused by both a neighbor (on numerous occasions) and a close family member (on two or three occasions).

My parents told me later that they were suspicious about the neighbor, but they never spoke about it. We moved to another town, and that was their way of dealing with it. So I never talked about it either: it was just our "family secret." As a result of the abuse, I determined that my value was in my body and that I had no control over what men did to me and that no one would fight for me. I was completely on my own.

When I got to high school, I was convinced that my sole value was in my body and my "performance." I was a major over-achiever. On the outside, I looked like I had it all together: straight A's, musical talent, and lots of friends. But inside I was a mess. I so wanted to be noticed, and I put a lot of emphasis on how guys saw me. After all, I was certain that my value was somehow tied up in my sexuality, and I had to prove that I was worth something.

My first two years of high school weren't terrible. I mostly just flirted a lot and allowed boys to occupy my thoughts. But in my junior year, I started making some dangerous decisions. Toward the end of my junior year, I ended up at a party with a guy I had been hoping would like me. In the pursuit of his affection, I was date-raped. I didn't call it that for a long time because I felt responsible. After all, I had put myself in a precarious position, but I had also very clearly said, "No," and he had very clearly said, "Whatever. I'll do what I want."

After that, I gave up on myself. I decided that since I had been sexually abused as a child and since now I wasn't even a virgin anymore, that I should just forget it and do whatever I felt like doing. Needless to say, I made a whole lot more bad decisions over the next two years.

I took a year off after high school and went to the Philippines as an exchange student. During that time, God started working on me, and in January of my freshman year of college, I accepted Christ. I didn't see it, but there was an immediate change in me. My roommates saw it, and so did my family—not all of them appreciated it a whole lot! I was really new in my faith, though, and I didn't know a whole lot about God's plan for sexuality.

A couple of months later, I started dating a guy who wasn't a Christian, and our relationship quickly became very physical. I didn't know there was anything wrong with having sex before you were married. I just didn't get it.

That summer I went to a Christian camp as just a helper. While I was there, I went with the girls to a "sex and dating" seminar, and for the first time, I heard about God's plan for sex, and I was blown away. I realized that I had been giving huge pieces of my heart away to whoever showed the slightest interest, and I had almost nothing left. But I also heard that God could forgive me and give me a clean slate. In fact, He already had done that the moment I had put my faith in Him. I heard God speaking to my heart saying, "You have to choose—me

56

or your boyfriend." I chose God. I broke up with my boyfriend and decided that I would not date anyone for at least a year.

Over the next few years, God did so much in me. I sought counseling from my pastor and was able to become free from a lot of the baggage in my past. God started changing my whole way of thinking about sexuality. I realized that what I had believed as a child was a lie. My value is in who I am in Christ. It has nothing to do with my body or performance. God is in total control, and I have the right to choose healthy relationships. And most important, yes, Someone did fight for me, and He fought to the death.

It's funny, as I matured in my faith and as I read and understood more and more of the Bible, the less I felt like dating. It just seemed like such a waste of time to me and really just a big temptation. I ended up not really dating anyone until I met my husband. When I met him, I knew he was the one God had chosen for me. I was right! He is amazing and perfect for me.

Our marriage has not always been easy. I discovered I still had some issues to work through, and we have had to work hard for intimacy in our relationship as a result of the choices both of us made. But God has blessed us as we have sought to honor Him first in our lives. We have children now, and my hope for them is that they will grow up with a healthy view of what God intends sexuality to be, and they will know that His plan is perfect and awesome.

My favorite verse in the Bible is Joel 2:25, "I will restore to you the years that the locust has eaten." I made so many bad choices in my life—some of them were forced on me, but many of them I chose willingly. It has not been an easy road, and I have so often wished I could go back and do it "right," but God has taken all of the junk and made me perfect and clean in Him. He has turned my mistakes into marks of grace. 🐚

twenty-one

I AM NOT CRAZY

Tom and I have been married for almost six months. We dated for eight years before we got married at the ages of 23 and 24, and we never had sex. We were told that we were crazy, that something was wrong with us, and that we were missing out on the "benefits."

Let me tell you something: our world is messed up!

Sex is not like it is in the movies. I always believed sex involved a permanent commitment and that it was an emotional and spiritual act. I have found out that I was right.

It was, and is, so great to know that Tom has never had another sexual partner. I am the only woman with whom he has shared that special bond—and vice versa.

I'm not going to tell you that Tom and I didn't give into temptation while we were dating. We did some things that we should have waited for, but we found that as long as we stayed close to God and His Word, it was much easier to stay pure.

Tom and I are enjoying getting to know each other physically and are excited to see all that God has planned for our future together. We're so glad we didn't listen to what everyone around us was saying.

twenty-two

ONE SNOWY NIGHT, MY LIFE CHANGED FOREVER

A little over a year ago, I stood with my husband underneath a prayer shawl in the redwoods as the minister spoke of the covering of God over our marriage. Leaves floated down around us, and songs and poems of loved ones flooded our ears. God had finally brought me my husband—the one for whom I had prayed and screamed and cried for so many years. This was the man that had been formed for me from the foundation of the earth and who is to walk by my side to the end of my days.

Things haven't always been this way.

In youth group on a Wednesday night when I was in tenth grade, I made my decision to save sex until marriage. The decision was not made out of any kind of spiritual fortitude or quest for holiness, but out of sheer unadulterated fear as a famous doctor looked me straight in the eye through the TV screen and told me I would get cervical cancer and die if I so much as thought about having sex before marriage.

By age 19, I had switched my reasoning more towards the spiritual fortitude route. Like most of the kids in Boulder, Colorado, I had gotten a crash course in beer, weed, and Buddhism, but I had grown tired of the scene and was now back at church and teaching Sunday school on the weekends.

One snowy night my life changed forever. My friend Jim's drunken roommate took what was supposed to have been for my husband, leaving me broken and sobbing on the floor of the shower. I watched as my purple hair dye swirled down the drain, wishing that the shameful deed that he had committed could be washed away too. A few weeks later, I learned I was pregnant. When he found out, he threatened me, saying I had to get an abortion. I told him I would, but I was lying. I decided to keep the baby, but I had a miscarriage early in the pregnancy. A month later, I was hospitalized for attempting suicide with my mother's anti-depressants.

From there, I traveled a long road of depression, bulimia, and the constant desire to end my life. I decided that I was damaged goods, and that none of the lovely Christian boys that my friends were all marrying would ever love me. So I kept company with a parade of co-dependent men that took what they wanted and threw me away. Some lasted a night, some a week, none for very long.

When I was 22, I got pregnant again, this time by a full-on, practicing Wiccan who was going through a bad divorce. I wanted to save him and fix him like all the others. When I told him I was pregnant, he told me he couldn't handle a child. I was left on my own to suffer through another painful miscarriage.

I thought that this was how I had to get a husband, and it was one after the other—a drug dealer, an alcoholic, a manic depressive. They were all guys who could never be the Godly man I really wanted. They were all just guys who took their piece of me and then threw me away. When I was 24, I was drugged and raped again, and I sank lower than I ever had before. All I could think was: "Who is stupid enough to let themselves get raped twice?"

I moved to California to start over. Eventually, God healed me enough to think that someday it might be possible to have the family of my dreams. I started living in a community where I was surrounded by men who loved me unconditionally and supported me. The chains started to drop away.

I dated a few Christian guys, but still they were all broken in some way. So I thought really hard about joining the orthodox convent near where I was living. Before I could finalize that decision, I had an opportunity to go to South Africa on a mission trip. I decided that the children I cared for there would be my children and that God would be my husband. I identified with Isaiah 61:10, "I delight greatly in the Lord; my soul rejoices in my God. For he has clothed me with garments of salvation and arrayed me in a robe of his righteousness as a bridegroom adorns his head like a priest and as a bride adorns herself with her jewels."

As I read these words, a great peace filled my heart. Throughout a two-year period in the beautiful country of South Africa with many beautiful people, I began to see the redemption that was to come from my tattered tale of love lost and taken.

In South Africa, the statistics of rape are staggering. One day, I held a four-year-old girl who had been brutalized by a man in her township. I whispered my story to her and told her that God heals the broken hearted and binds their wounds.

So many times on that trip, I gathered up all the strength that I had in me, and I got up in front of the 50 or so girls that sat around my feet, and I told them my story. Their beautiful brown eyes would go wide in disbelief as this white girl from California shared with them the same hurts that they carried—most of them in silence as is the custom of the culture. They couldn't believe that this had happened to anyone else, much less the American who had traveled so far to be with them. I hugged them and cried with them, and we were healed together in a way that I couldn't have imagined years before when the skies were so dark.

I went back home to raise funds and get a visa to move to South

Africa permanently. Two weeks later, I met the man who was to be my husband.

I struggled for months to tell him about my past. Every week like clockwork, I would break down and cry and tell him that he couldn't really love me if he knew what I had done and what I had been through. When I finally told him, he said it didn't matter. He said it was in the past and that he loved me and cared so deeply about me. He said he was sorry that others had hurt me. He doesn't mind that I may never be able to have children because of the attacks I endured. He wept with me earlier this year as I lost another child that was to be ours. He sees other children in our future, children that were born to other parents and who are now given to us to love and raise.

We live in Portland, Oregon, which has one of the highest rates of sex trafficking and child prostitution in the country. I am currently in training to speak in high schools about the sexual assault and prostitution that plagues our city.

In an effort to bring God's healing to those who have been hurt as I was, I will keep telling my story until my days on this earth are done.

Whatever your story, please know that there is hope and redemption through the love of God. 🐚

twenty-three

I LOVE MY GIRLFRIEND, BUT I LOVE GOD MORE

When I realized the magnitude of a relationship with God and subsequently rededicated my life to Him, part of that for me was a promise not to have sex until marriage. This includes not just sex but anything beyond kissing that would arouse the natural urge inside me.

When I first started wearing a promise ring in high school, I was a little afraid of how people would respond. I thought I might be mocked. And sure enough, I was asked, "What are you gay?" or "Oh, you're some kind of a prude Christian!" However, there weren't as many as I thought there would be. In fact, most people who know of my decision have expressed their admiration and respect.

I'm not saying it's easy to make a commitment to purity and that once you make that promise the devil backs off and admits defeat. No, if anything he only doubles his efforts to defeat you. In high school, I was offered room keys on various trips and asked in some subtle and not-so-subtle ways if I wanted to "have fun," but I'm proud to say I didn't given in. That wasn't because I'm some super human with an incredibly strong will. It was because I prayed extremely hard in those situations, and God always gave me the strength to do the right thing.

God isn't watching from above, waiting for me to mess up. He's right there with me, waiting to help.

I'm now in my junior year of college, and I've been dating someone for the past two years. Believe me when I say that once you start dating someone you care about, the temptation only gets worse. I love this girl with all my heart; I truly do. But the one thing I always focus on is that I love God more. Thankfully, she has her heart set on Him first and foremost too. But that's not to say we don't get tempted. We're away at college, and it's easy to think that no one would know. I get pressure from society and friends, trying to tell me what we "need" to do. We've ignored all that, and you should too.

From the beginning when we started dating, we were intentional in creating boundaries for ourselves, boundaries that we promised God and each other we would respect. And this has been huge in helping us maintain integrity and purity as a couple. We make it a point to focus on God together.

Again though, I know that temptation will come, and in addition to our commitment, I have accountability partners. There is strength in numbers!

So take encouragement and know that God will be with you in your relationships if you make it a point to focus on Him. Whoever you are reading this, know that I am in prayer for you. You are not alone in this, and you can do this! 🤜

twenty-four

I HAD TO LEARN TO TRUST

After having been married for not even six months, I can tell you that sex is an amazing and wonderful gift that God designed for a husband and wife. I want to share some of my story with you.

At a pretty pivotal time in my own development as a woman, my dad had a series of affairs with other women and eventually divorced my mom. As a 17-year-old, trying to get an understanding of who I was as a woman, this deeply impacted my view of myself. I had a really low opinion of myself, feeling somehow responsible for some of what happened.

I began believing that there was no way for me to trust other men and that what happened to my mom would probably eventually happen to me. While all of this was going on, I met a guy that I really liked. He began pursuing me. This felt great to me because it gave me a temporary sense of self-worth. The only problem was that it was exactly that—temporary. He wasn't a Christian, and although I had told myself I would never date someone who didn't have the same values as I did, I really wanted something to help me feel better about myself. This seemed like the answer at the time. Since our values were so different, he had a totally different idea about sex and everything surrounding it.

During this time I pushed every boundary I had ever set up for myself. I pulled away from God, and isolated myself from everyone around me who loved me. Although my boyfriend and I never had sex, we crossed boundaries sexually that God had designed only for marriage. And because we weren't meant to be so intimate with one another, it had a painful impact on my life. I became more and more dissatisfied with myself. I could not stand who I had become. I hated looking at myself in the mirror. I felt guilty, out of control, unloved by God, and unable to pull myself out of the situation.

Well, God always loves us unconditionally despite our mistakes and our disobedience. He is a God of restoration. He always gives us a way out. I felt trapped in the relationship, but God gave me a way out. I broke up with this boyfriend and went to Nyack College in New York.

After breaking up with him, God gave me a beautiful two years of being single. During this time, I became much more confident in who I was in Christ. I feel like God spent those two years healing my heart from all the pain that misused sexuality had brought me—both mine and my father's. I no longer felt shame about the things I had done but was able to accept responsibility and receive forgiveness. I also learned how to forgive myself.

At the end of my sophomore year, I began dating the guy who is now my husband. We dated for two years and were married this past June. Through Jay, God has shown me a new kind of love. This love is truly unselfish, doesn't seek lustful things, and it feels right! Jay always encourages me to be a better person. He empowers me and always treats me as a woman of value and worth. After believing for a long time that I would always have to earn a love that won't ever let go, I have learned to trust in God to hold our relationship together.

As a married couple, we are able to connect through sex on a level that is even deeper. We are able to express our love to each other in a way that we can't with anybody else. It is a precious thing that is powerful.

I am so grateful that when we had sex on our wedding night, we hadn't shared that experience with anybody else. I am also grateful that there is healing, restoration, and forgiveness when we do make mistakes. I have made my share of them, but it is always better if we can learn from the mistakes of others rather than make the mistakes ourselves. It is hard in a society like ours to totally understand what sex is all about. I honestly didn't completely understand until I got married and experienced it as God designed it to be.

twenty-five

I MADE A PACT
WITH MY BOYFRIEND

My boyfriend and I both realized that it was important to set certain boundaries for each other. For example, we could kiss but not too much. We could hug but not for extended periods. We also made a pact that when we watched movies and television, we would never lie down next to one another. We were able to recognize temptation and make new plans. We never had sex or even came close for that matter, but we pushed the kissing thing a bit. It is important to know that you can always come back to God even when you've failed. God is good and kind.

For my own part, I was committed even before I was in a relationship to keeping myself pure for my future husband. I think the commitment is important. I also think it is important to be aware of the need for self-control through prayer. It is hard at times, but God is our strength, and He will definitely help us. We need to focus our minds on Him. We can't focus on lust. We need to keep our minds pure by focusing on Him.

A verse that encourages me to remain pure is Philippians 4:8, *"Finally, brothers, whatever is true, whatever is noble, whatever is right, whatever is pure, whatever is lovely, whatever is admirable—if anything is excellent or praiseworthy—think about such things."*

Ultimately, I'm glad and thankful that God helped me stay pure in my dating relationship. He has blessed me. 🖐

twenty-six

I HAD TO LEARN TO FORGIVE MY HUSBAND

U nlike my husband, I didn't grow up in a Christian home. My family didn't tell me to wait until I was married to have sex. No one really talked about it. I distinctly remember getting into a conversation with my aunt about sex when I was in college. She was shocked when I told her I was a virgin. She told me she thought I was crazy! She encouraged me to sleep with my boyfriend to see if we were compatible in the bedroom. She said I should sleep with as many people as I could before settling down in order to get experience.

At that point in my life, I already knew I was going to wait until I was married before having sex. I accepted the Lord as my personal Savior in seventh grade, and because of that decision, I made a vow to remain pure until my wedding day. So, naturally when I was talking to my aunt that day, I thought she was the crazy one! I've come to find out, though, that so many people find it completely acceptable to sleep with one, two, four, ten, or more people with absolutely no regard to how it will affect their future.

Fast forward a few years: I fell in love with Dave whom I would eventually marry. The more we got to know each other, the more I grew to love him. I remember the exact time and place he told me he wasn't a virgin. I remember immediately feeling like something was taken from me, and, looking back, it was. I intentionally saved myself for my husband and just sort of assumed he would do the same for me.

When we got engaged, I really had to work through my emotions and feelings toward Dave about his past sexual life. I felt cheated, betrayed (even though it had happened before we met), upset, angry, disappointed—so many things. It wasn't an easy road toward healing, but with Jesus as the center of our relationship, the healing we both so desperately needed eventually found us.

So what does that look like practically? There were many long, honest talks. There were tons of tears, prayers, and talking with other people we trusted. I was finally able to accept his apology and extend the forgiveness he needed. It's been a huge blessing to allow God to help us through that tough place.

So, can God redeem even the most broken relationship? Of course He can, but we play such a huge part of the story as well. Do you know how much heartache would've been saved for both Dave and me if we had been able to come together in complete purity?

I know in high school and sometimes even in college, it's hard to imagine the person you're going to marry. For some of you, marriage seems like an eternity away, but speaking from experience, it's going to come a whole lot faster than you think. Save yourself and your future spouse the heartache and commit to remaining pure until your wedding day. I guarantee you'll bring a lot less baggage into your marriage if you do. 🤜

twenty-seven

WE ARE SO THANKFUL
WE WAITED

Her Story

I'm just so thankful that God protected both of us from having sex before we were married. I can't imagine sharing something so intimate and vulnerable with someone else. I think I would have a hard time if I had waited and Ben hadn't, knowing that he had shared that intimacy with someone else. There is something incredibly beautiful and intimate about experiencing sex for the first time as marriage partners.

Ben's decision to wait until marriage to have sex proves a deep level of self-control that makes me that much more confident in his commitment to me and his fidelity. I truly believe that sex has wrongly been made to be the goal of a relationship when God really gave it to us as a part of a marriage relationship to complement the emotional and spiritual connection between two people. 🎺

His Story

When I was in high school, I thought that sex would be by far the most important part of my future marriage. I heard older, married people talk about how sex was really a very small part of marriage, and I thought they were crazy. But after being married for six years, I realize that it really is not the most important part of my marriage.

In our society, sex has come to be viewed as one of the most important aspects of a relationship. This has really distorted our ability to relate to members of the opposite sex. We were created to be in a relationship with God and with others, but we have come to view sex as the only aspect of a relationship. Although people I know in high school wouldn't admit it, I know that sex is often the driving factor in their dating relationships and even in their friendships.

One thing I'd say to guys is that we often think that the real sign of manhood is having sex, but the truth is that real men are asked by God to treat women with respect, love, and honor. A real man is one who is willing to love a woman for who she is and wait to have sex with her until he is willing to pledge himself to her for his life. Girls are used to seeing their value in their bodies and their sexual nature instead of looking for men who will love them for who they are. 👊

twenty-eight

I DIDN'T WANT TO FOLLOW THE CROWD

A s far back as I can remember, I was girl-crazy. I remember getting in trouble in preschool for kissing a girl. Through elementary and middle school, I always had a "girlfriend." By girlfriend, I mean someone I talked to on the phone. Occasionally, my mom would take us to play miniature golf or attend a church function or something like that.

As I grew older and could drive, I can remember specifically thinking that I wanted to keep myself from crossing certain lines with girls. I wanted to save myself for marriage. I didn't want to push the limits and be just another guy who was looking for one thing with girls. I wanted to follow God's plan for sex within marriage only.

I know now that it was God who gave me this desire. It was God who gave me the strength to pursue my goal to be a real man in this area. Many of my friends weren't making the same decision, but I wanted to be a man of God and knew that sex before marriage wasn't an option. I decided to draw lines that I would not cross because I knew that if I did, it would be downhill from there.

Besides wanting to be a real man of God, I had a strong desire to offer my future wife the gift and respect of waiting. I continually asked

God for His strength to remain strong. It was only because of God and His strength that I was able to remain true to my goal. I want you to know that it was not because of my own ability. It was only because of His strength.

I occasionally put myself in dangerous places. If I had not been reminded of what was expected of me and if I did not have clear goals, the outcomes could have been very sad.

As I entered college, I was just as girl-crazy as ever. The difference was that I was on my own away from home. I came to college excited about many things, including the girls that I would meet. I had no idea that I would meet *the* girl. I met Julia during freshmen orientation. We hit it off right away. Eventually, God made a way for us to enter into a dating relationship.

When we were dating, Julia and I had open, candid conversations. Talking about sexual boundaries and being on the same page saved us frustration, confusion, and pain. The result was that we were able to give each other the gifts God intended for us to be able to give. This is a great source of health in our marriage as we were able to unite without a lot of pain and baggage. God can help couples work through that pain, of course, but we understand the wisdom of His plan for sex within marriage. Our wedding day was truly amazing, unbelievable, and God-inspired.

That is my story. I hope that it encourages you to make good decisions and lean on God for strength and perseverance. Waiting and saving yourself for marriage is more than worth any struggles you may have.

— Jeff Pearson

twenty-nine

WE CAN TELL YOU HOW TO LIVE WITHOUT REGRET

We are happy to have the opportunity to contribute to this book that Julia, our daughter, originally wrote for her Young Life kids. Jeff and Julia love their kids enough to tell them the truth, which is that God's plan is best, not only for your life now, but for the long haul. Sex is an amazing gift that God gives to two people to enjoy within the marriage relationship. Deep inside, you all know that, but sometimes you decide not to believe it for yourselves. Hopefully the stories in this book will help you embrace the truth that will set you free!

When we were dating, we chose to believe for ourselves that God's plan was best. Not only did we commit not to have sex before marriage, but we made the choice not even to kiss until we got engaged! You might think that's a little extreme, but here's the thing: thirty-three years later, we don't have even one tiny little regret that we made that commitment and stuck to it.

And that's the consequence we want to talk to you about—regret. What is regret? It's an awful feeling in your mind and your heart and your gut that comes to plague you when you make a poor decision. You've had regret about small decisions for sure. It's that feeling you get when you know you shouldn't have had the fifth piece of pizza, but you do it anyway. Well, that regret will disappear by the next morning when your stomach is growling again! The regret that comes when you choose to give your body to someone you're not married to—that kind of regret lasts a lifetime. God will forgive you, sure, but regret is a consequence that will stay with you, and it will impact your life in so many harmful ways.

We've been around for more than 50 years now—more than 100 years if you add us together! We've worked with thousands of people throughout the course of 30 years of ministry. Here's the truth. We've never known anyone who chose to have sex before marriage who hasn't lived with regret about that. And we've never known anyone— including ourselves—who has ever regretted choosing to wait.

So there's a no-brainer. Have sex now, and you'll be one hundred percent guaranteed to have major regrets about it afterwards. Wait to enjoy God's gift of sex until after you're married, and you're one hundred percent guaranteed not to regret it. In fact, the older you get, the more you'll understand why waiting was the best decision you ever made!

— Rev. Marty and Laurie Berglund

A Message from Julia

This book is a collection of personal, intimate stories. For me and for every other contributor, there is something very beautiful about believing that by sharing our trials, failures, successes, miscalculations, and bright ideas, we can be helpful to you. Believing that you can gain insight and help in making good choices in your own very personal decisions is what has inspired us to reveal so much about ourselves.

As you have read in our stories, we all fall far short of perfection. It may seem to you that some fell further than others, but the truth is that to God, it is all imperfection. In the Bible in Romans 3:23, it says, *"For all have sinned and fall short of the glory of God."* God is good and perfect, and we are not. We have all chosen to sin in big and small ways. We all fall short of His perfection.

God, the God of the Holy Bible, is a loving and generous Father who created us to be in a relationship with Him. How can that happen when we all fall short of what He wants us to be? It can't happen on our own. No matter how hard we try, we can't be perfect on our own.

We are stuck in an impossible situation where sin gets in the way of our relationship with God—the relationship we were created to have. So the Father in all His radical love made the ultimate sacrifice as a solution to our broken relationship with him. He sent His son to die for us.

81

Romans 3:23-24 (NCV) says: *"God makes people right with himself through their faith in Jesus Christ. This is true for all who believe in Christ, because all people are the same: All have sinned and are not good enough for God's glory, and all need to be made right with God by his grace, which is a free gift. They need to be made free from sin through Jesus Christ."*

God's free gift was the only perfect sacrifice. Jesus, the same little baby who was born in a manger, was sent to earth with the most incredible plan of all time—to live a sinless life that was so powerful that we are still talking about it thousands of years later—and to die on a cross in order to be a sacrifice for our sins. This one act was God's plan to fix our relationship with him. Jesus' sacrifice bridges the gap in our relationship with God and allows us to be in right relationship with Him.

How does this relate to sex and to mistakes and purity and all of our stories? It says in 2 Corinthians 5:17, *"If anyone is in Christ, they are a new creation. The old has gone the new has come."*

Everyone who contributed to this book believes this. God takes the mess that has been made of our lives, whether by our own sin or someone else's, and He wipes it clean. We bring it to Him, and He makes us a new creation. That is why we can uncover it all because we are confident that Christ's death has washed our sins away, and we know that a relationship with God is the only answer in this life.

Titus 3:5-6 says, *"He saved us because of his mercy. It was not because of good deeds we did to be right with him. He saved us through the washing that made us new people through the Holy Spirit. God poured out richly upon us that Holy Spirit through Jesus Christ our Savior."*

I know that the thought of "starting a relationship" with the God of the universe can seem daunting, but it's truly so simple. It is just letting God know in a simple prayer that you are forever grateful for the gift of Jesus and that you want to follow Him with your whole life.

From there, reach out to the reaching hand of God, and you will begin your new journey with Him by your side.

So above all, my greatest prayer regarding this book is that you would know the truth of the sacrifice made for you and that you would walk with joy and passion in your relationship with God because of the freedom Christ Jesus has given you. 🎨